# Along the Way

# Deborah Thatcher Robbins

**ALONG THE WAY**

First Edition
Printed in the USA

Wtrsgn1@gmail.com
Sixtyandstillstunning.net

Editor: Alisha Sanders
Cover Photo: Shaun & Sarah Reardon
Author's Assistants: Zach Robbins, Josh White, Sarah Reardon, Mary Linda Thatcher Ripley, Jody Reed, Averie Robbins and Jonah Robbins
Page Photos: Deborah Thatcher Robbins

All writings and quotes are written by Deborah Thatcher Robbins

**This book is dedicated to my family and
friends who never stopped believing in me!
Thank you for your love and support!**

To my children, Sarah E. Reardon, Joshua F. White, and Zachary D.M. Robbins, you all are my reason and my constant source of love and inspiration.

To my two wonderful sisters, Mary Linda Thatcher Ripley and Jody Reed, you have never left my side and have always cheered me on with your love and guidance. Words can't express how blessed I feel having you both in my life!

To my children's families: Sean Reardon (son-in-law), Amy Alvis White (daughter-in-law), and Lynsey Robbins (daughter-in-law). Thank you for always being understanding and supportive to my children as they lovingly go along with some of my crazy, creative ideas and my coming to "visit" for extended amounts of time; it means so much to me.

To my grandchildren, Becca White, Jackson White, Jonah Robbins, Averie Robbins, Emma Reardon, and Taylor Peterson. You all are happily a source for many of my writings with your unending energy, bright, beautiful souls, and joyful hearts.

To some very precious friends in my life, Diane T. Morgan, you have been a lifeline for me through much of my life! Thank you for always being there for me! Sherry D. Manley, you have always been there for me through many years and many changes. Thank you!

Katherine Parkes, always just a phone call away! Many years of friendship, love and support; thank you! Nonie Iliffe Fajao, near to a lifetime as friends, so blessed to have your love! Lucinda Slade Johnson, my sister from another mother! My beach buddy, always supportive and loving!

To so many wonderful friends that have been more like family to me; you know who you are. I am truly blessed to have you all walking this path with me and being part of the contents of this beautiful book, *Along the Way*. Thank you!

# CONTENTS

So much of my journey has been feeling my way through, like walking down a wooded path and having to push through the branches so that I could continue. We can't let the branches that we encounter along our path stop us from continuing our journey. Sometimes the branches are there to remind us to slow down, be careful, have strength and be aware. The branches are also there to inspire us to push on! My wish with this book as I bend another branch forward, is to share with you words of wisdom, hope and love that you will be inspired to follow your dreams no matter how many branches you must push through, "Along the Way!"

# Be

Find joy in the little things, capture each moment in your heart, dare to let yourself dream, and be happy right from the start!

# Your Strength

Sometimes your strength has a way of sneaking out of your eyes in the form of tiny water droplets.

# Bloom Wherever You Want To

Bloom wherever you want to, wherever it feels good!

# Anything Is Possible

Awaken to this new day, fresh with unlimited opportunity, and know that anything is possible with faith, love, and determination.

# Aging Beautifully

Aging beautifully is a state of mind, not a mirror reflection!

# The Quiet Of The Morning

Ahhhh, yes. In the quiet of the morning, through the darkness of the night past, she silently crept… with a twinkling of first light. Slowly, the sky displayed magnificent colors of blues, pinks, and yellows… and then, like magic, she appeared out from behind the mountains. Her entrance, as graceful as a swan… and as with every performance, she brought with her gifts of light and warmth for all of us to share!

# Truly Blessed

The sun is shining, the birds are singing, the sky is blue, the air is clear, and I'm alive and able to take part in this beautiful new day! Truly blessed!

# She Knew There Was More

She knew there was more, she could feel it. She knew that in her wonderings she would find it, someday!

# Affairs Of the Heart

Be the manager of your life. If someone that you previously hired as a co-worker isn't doing their job, give them their pink slip, time to rehire

# My Mother

As I approach the age of what my mother was when I started to worry about her being okay, thinking that she was old, I look back and I wonder if I loved her enough. I wonder if I showed her that I cared enough. I wonder if I spent enough time with her, being a part of her life! I hope the answers to these questions are yes because I know how much she loved me and how happy she was when we were together! I know how much her children and grandchildren meant to her. I know how much she meant to me, and I sure hope that I showed it. I would give it all for one more moment with this wonderful woman.

# But Only for A Moment

You know that feeling you get in the middle of the night… that one that sometimes is too hard to fight… when the ache just won't go away.

We toss and turn and find some comfort in a position that reminds us of a time when the warmth of love held us close… and we let our minds wander to that time… but only for a moment.

And in the silence of the night, we weep.

We have conditioned ourselves to become numb when thoughts of love and happiness come our way, armor for our fragile hearts… accepting that love will never be again, and we still wonder why… but only for a moment…

# The Best Medicine

Do you know in my opinion and experience what the best medicines are in the whole wide world? Family, love, laughter, and friends! A spoonful of that every day helps to keep the doctors away!

# The Voice Within You

Listen to the voice within you; it's the power behind your dreams. You have taken steps in the right direction, and you must continue!

# I Am My Courage

I am not my past. I am not my mistakes, losses, or missed opportunities. I am what I have overcome. I am my courage, strength and loving heart.

# Find The Glue

If the pieces of yesterday are worth putting back together, by all means, find the glue!

# Blue

I am thankful for the first light of day that softly finds its way through my window every morning! I am thankful for my children, my family and my friends. I am thankful for my continued good health. I am thankful for the sweet callings of a distant bird awakening to this new day! I am thankful for the people that I pass by every day on my walk that return my smile and a friendly hello! I am thankful for the handsome Blue Heron that I once met not so long ago that I named Blue! Blue and I would meet every morning at the water's edge, and we would share each other's company for what seemed like hours. I did most of the talking, Blue did all the listening!

# Enjoy This New Day

A hush came over the crowd, the birds and I, the theater grew brighter and brighter, and our hearts were pounding faster. All eyes were on the stage. Suddenly, there she was, the miraculous star that she is. So bright and beautiful as she rose in an effortless dance that brought the audience to their feet as we applauded with words of thanks (me) and songs of joy (the birds!) Enjoy this new day!

# Let's Leave Our Words Unsaid

Be still with me for a moment; let's leave our words unsaid. In the silence, hear our heartbeats counting every breath instead.

# With Every Step

I've noticed, with physical pain, that if I don't let it stop me and I keep on moving, with every step the pain lessens. I believe the same is true when your heart is full of pain, if you don't let it stop you and you keep on moving, with every step the pain will lessen!

# A Precious Gift

This morning, the air was cool as the birds, and I watched and waited for our star to arrive. Whoever did the lighting for the pre-show did an awesome job using soft hues of pink, orange, yellow and blue. Suddenly, she appeared moving with great speed onto her stage, up, up, up, over the mountains, brilliant and as flawless as ever! The dawning of a new day! A precious gift that I am thankful for always! Oh, and I would like to thank whoever did the backdrop for the show, too; simply amazing!

# Being Yourself

It's not about finding yourself; you are right there. You haven't gone anywhere! It's about being yourself. You can't run away from yourself and find yourself; it makes no sense! Yourself will always be there!

Try being yourself and stop trying to find something that's not lost!

# Just Me and My Bike

Just me and my bike enjoying the transition from light to night. The night sky put on quite a show, and the surrounding area performed with dancing reflections like mirror images— my favorite time to practice conscious realizations and unspoken gratitude.

# Kindness Matters

My witty wisdom for today is. Don't always be looking for a pat on the back! If you are truly trying to do good, just do it and people will notice. If you are proclaiming it, you better be able to back it up! People will want to see results! Be aware that, trying to do good becomes a lie if people are getting hurt in your endeavor! Kindness matters, always and to everyone!

# A Difference of Opinion

We have differences in opinion, but I am still human. My heart beats like yours; we are born into human form, so our similarities of body and our creation are the same. Our only differences are our eyes and how we see things! From there, we tell ourselves to think from what we see and oftentimes, we allow others to tell us how we should see things! When I see you, I see another beautiful human being that I am always open to knowing and caring about, another person that I have a chance to interact with in a thoughtful, caring way! Even if you see things differently than me, my hopes are always that you will see me as I am and then tell yourself, "This is another beautiful human that I am open to knowing and caring about, even if she sees things differently than I do." Imagine what the world would be like if we looked at each other with loving eyes!

# Fix It

So the way I look at it is, don't rely on the saying " if it's meant to be it will be!"
Instead, put faith in yourself and "if it's not happening, fix it!"

# All I Ask

All I ask of you is that you use kind words when you speak to me, please! I am a strong woman, but I've been through a lot, and I have feelings. Say unto others as you would have others say unto you! I ask this in love and peace!

# In The Process

When you're in the process of getting where you are going, sometimes once you get there, it's not at all where you thought you would be!

# Live For Today

Rose early this morning to see the rising sun, looked all around me to see the wonders that God had done. Felt the morning breeze caress my sleepy face, watched the snowflakes fall to earth, like little bits of lace. Live for today, while you can, take the time to understand, life's too short, don't let it slip away. Walked along the cold white snow, that gathered at my feet, sharing nature's miracles, made me feel so complete. Spoke three words I love you, sometimes that's all it takes, to put a smile on someone's face, what a difference it can make. Live for today, while you can take the time to understand, life's too short, don't let it slip away. Touch a snowflake, wish on a star, take the time no matter who you are, life's too short, don't let it slip away.

# Don't Forget Who You Are

Don't forget who you are! You are a gentle soul, and you must not let those with over-exuberant personalities overpower your space or make you feel inadequate in any way! Your gentleness is unique and part of who you are. You are a master in your field; don't forget that. And don't forget all the accolades and praises that have come your way. This new field has a different system of planting. It may take some time to learn the system and get the seeds in the ground, but when the fruit matures, it will be beautiful! Keep your shoulders back and your head held high!

# Emerge As You

Give yourself a chance to discover how wonderful life can be! There is so much yet unknown, unrealized, unfelt, undone, untouched, and unseen. There is a whole world out there waiting for you to emerge as you!

# Morning Star

The morning air was crisp and still and silence was abound, the cooing of some distant birds was the only sound. Darkened mountains in the midst and dark skies growing bright, all we're waiting patiently to see the first light. Then beyond the mountain tops and over fields of green, a little glimmer of days first light could suddenly be seen. There she was the morning star in her bright and shiny way, bringing us a special gift of this glorious new day.

# The Key to Happiness

I think the key to being happy is different for everyone. What makes one person happy might not work for another person! There is no magic wand that people wave around, and then they are happy. I also think happiness does not come from within as many quotes would have you believe. To me, and for as long as I have known myself, happiness comes from being around people you love and who love you in return. The interaction you have with these people brings happiness, a feeling of contentment (which is a word used to define happiness in the dictionary) and joy! So, I believe we receive happiness from other people; it's not something that we just bring forth from inside of us.

I believe other people are the trigger for happiness or sadness. Our lives are full of interactions with other people on a day-to-day basis, and how that interaction unfolds will determine how we feel! So essentially, other people set the stage for how we react and whether it is happy or not. Life events play a role in happiness as well. People will say, "Well, you have to embrace where you are in your life and be grateful for what you have." I agree with that statement to a certain extent in that, yes, being grateful for what you have at that moment is important. However, it shouldn't make you complacent, feeling that that is all there is. Being grateful shouldn't make you feel like you have arrived at the end of your road or stop you from continuing to reach for the happiness, contentment and joy you thirst for! As my life continues to unfold, I realize that the happiest time of my life was when I was raising my children. I was surrounded by people who loved me, and that made me happy. Now, as I am aging and traveling alone, I seek that feeling of happiness again.

I'm not an expert on how life should be lived to be happy, but I do know what works for me, and that is being around people I love and who love me.

# Those Precious Moments

In love (when there is a broken relationship), why is there so much pain when there is so much pleasure to be had?

What makes us forget those precious moments that brought our hearts together? What makes us forget our love?

# Move Mountains

If you really want something, you will move mountains to get it!

# Beautiful Awakening

Every day is a beautiful awakening to life! I am grateful for this new day.

# Your Silence

Your silence tells me more than I want to hear!

# Monday

Maybe if we celebrate Monday like we do Friday, we could have a much better day and week! Let's try it… Yippee it's Monday! Have a happy Monday! TGIM, didn't think it would ever get here! Been such a long weekend, so happy it's finally Monday! I don't know about how you feel, but it just doesn't feel the same to me. Well at least we tried!

# Unsung Heroes

Stepparents are unsung heroes! They have agreed to take someone else's child into their lives and hearts and love them like their own. Here's to all the stepparents out there! Thank you for all you do and all that you have sacrificed for someone else's child.

# A New Chapter

First light! Let this new day be the beginning of a new chapter in your story! Full of new opportunities to seek and receive the beautiful life you were meant to have! Step forward into this chapter with confidence and purpose, knowing that what is waiting for you is more wonderful than you could have ever imagined!

# I Speak to The Moon

Lying here in bed tonight in the darkness of my room, I noticed a muted hue of pale, yellow light coming through my half-open blinds. As I walked over to the window, I pulled the blinds aside, and my eyes were quickly drawn upwards to the sky and the magnificent full moon! I have always felt a connection to the moon, and tonight is no different. I speak to the moon like it is a person, and it hears everything I say! There is a mystery about the moon, yet I feel its power and strength when I am in its presence. In the moments before I fall asleep as the moonbeams cascade across my bed, I feel comfort within me and a feeling that all is well! Sleep tight!

# Life Choices

Life choices sometimes might not turn out the way you expected or hoped that they would, but all are very necessary for the process of getting you to where you need to be! I'm still on my journey!

# Just Be There When They Ask

Do I feel obligated or somehow meant to be the gatekeeper? Is my readiness for connection with loved ones more than just my love for them? Does it also have to do with being a mom and having that everlasting, motherly need to nurture and take care of everyone? Do I have sleepless nights because I'm going over in my mind what-ifs and thinking, "Maybe if I'm there, everything will be okay, so I better be there!" I have that constant wave of wishing that comes over me to be everywhere at once and with all my children to make sure everyone is okay, when, they already are!

Can I, as a mother, ever realize that as much as I want to save everyone, ultimately, they will all have to save themselves, just like I had to do? Can I finally realize that I have raised my children well, and that they are able to care for themselves? Do I need to have more confidence in them or me? I think the answer is me! Am I willing to easily say, "What I don't know won't hurt me," or does that make me feel more eager to put the landing pad underneath them, just in case!? Do I feel that my adult children need to know what mom thinks would be best for them? Yes, I do, and it's very hard to let that go, to stay silent and walk away! As mothers of adult children, we should realize that we are no longer supplying the worms so they can eat or still giving them flying lessons. We have raised our little birds to fly strong, and they have earned their wings! They learned from me, so they already know everything that I might feel the need to say while they stand there rolling their eyes! We must now watch our adult birds fly and stay supportive while knowing that they will be okay! Just be there when they ask!

# Make A Promise to Yourself

Going back to what hurt you and made you leave is not the answer. Give yourself some time. Your current situation isn't the end of the story. It's not easy right now, and you feel unsettled and out of place, but that is just temporary. Get yourself out and about to meet people and network. Put some effort into creating the life you want. Don't get pulled back by old habits because it is familiar and easier. Make a promise to yourself to never accept less than you deserve, never allow someone else to mistreat you, and above all, feel good about yourself. Know your worth and get excited about the possibilities! You have a special reason to be here on earth, and it is not to suffer and be a sacrificial lamb. Let yourself become the lioness you were meant to be and roar!

# How You Handle the Load

It's not what you carry along your journey, it's how you handle the load!

# I Don't Know

I don't know. It doesn't matter if I know; I don't have to know! Eventually, I will know!

# Gathered Moments

As the sun was slowly setting in the sky of crimson red, my feet were swishing through the leaves and crunching where I tread.

The slightest chill of evening air I felt upon my face, a mourning dove's familiar call from a not- too-distant place.

A moment of awareness in the vastness of time. Gathered moments that I can call mine.

# The Stage Was Set

The stage was set with beautiful mountain backdrops. Green, lush alfalfa fields, palm trees swaying in the morning breeze, a distant cooing from a mourning dove, and a scattering of fluffy, white clouds. Certainly, it must have taken years to put that all together! Anyway, we (the birds and I) were ready and patiently waiting for the show to begin. Some of us were a little anxious (the birds kept flying around and wouldn't stay in their seats!) Suddenly, the house lights grew brighter, up came the curtain, and there she was, just as she always is, bright, beautiful and shining. A true star! Enjoy your gift of a sunny new day!

# Not For the Faint of Heart

Love is a fleeting emotion that can change in an instant. Love comes with no guarantees but many promises! Love is not for the faint at heart and should be entered into with no expectations!

# Just One Moment

Please, surrender yourself for just one moment to breathe in the aroma of the fresh morning air. Feel the breeze as it gently caresses your face. Touch the tiny droplets of morning dew held on little sprigs of grass. Listen to the sounds of silence and stand in awe of life's miracles! Grateful for this new day!

# He Never Lets Me Down

He never lets me down when I really need Him. He just shows me sometimes that I can also save myself.

# Hit The Ball Out of The Park

I'm not going to steal a base when the bases are loaded, with the chance of getting out before I reach home! I'm going to wait until the ball is hit out of the park, and then we all get home safely!

# In The Stillness
## of The Early Morn

In the stillness of the early morn, as the sun took center stage, I was once again so thankful to be given this brand-new page. Another day to write my story, another day to live, another day to be aware of all that life has to give; the smallest things like birds in flight, the crisp fresh morning air, sparkling dewdrops, cooing doves, are all gifts of life to share. To be aware and present in the story that you write. Use all your senses: hear, touch, smell, taste, and sight!

# Seekers Of Contentment

Seekers of contentment, do what ultimately will make you happy! So much time is wasted and lost trying to figure everything out. Just do what you want to do! And when the naysayers come hovering around, smile, and continue your quest, it's so easy!

# Your Reality

Your reality might not be quite what you thought it would be at this stage of the game, but you are still here, and it is never too late to make things how you want them to be. Stay strong, stay focused, stay vigilant, and stay on course.

If you come upon a bend in the road, walk in the middle, where it is usually higher ground. Always keep your faith in a higher power leading you through your journey where ultimately, you will find your miracles and the life you have always longed for!

# A Higher Power

It has been a while since I have shared this space with the mountains and palm trees. Here in the desert, you become aware that there is something much greater, a feeling of spiritual wholeness and connection with a higher power, a knowingness.

# Stay True to Yourself

Everyone will have their own opinion of you, but only you have the inside scoop! Stay true to yourself!

# Like

Like is very important in a loving relationship.

# We All Have Your Back

If you are going through a time in your life that you struggle with, not knowing which way to go, feeling alone and confused, stop, take a couple of deep breaths and remember the bird that seems like it is following you that you see all the time and how you find pennies every now and then or hear the same song repeatedly. Those are all signs from your guardian angels to let you know that you are not alone and that they are right there with you! You know that feeling at the pit of your stomach when things don't feel right, that is God's way of letting you know He is watching over you and guiding you to change the things that don't feel right. Remember the connection with family that you have near and far that would go to the ends of the earth for you. Think about the true friends you have that would be at your side in a blink of an eye! So don't ever feel like you are alone because you are not, you have family, friends, God, and your angels, and we all have your back!

# Settle Into Your Sleeping Place

Settle into your sleeping place and let your troubles go. Tomorrow is another day to live, love, and grow.

# The First Step

The first step is always the hardest to take. The second step can be hard too, but once you get in that forward motion, one foot in front of the other, you begin to feel a sense of accomplishment and pride in yourself. You smile because you had the courage to change your life, and all it took was that voice inside you saying, "It's time."

# Empty Arms

I have always given myself to the first bidder; the first to show an interest, the first to welcome me with a smile, the first to make me feel wanted. Allowing myself to do this in desperation for love and companionship has almost always resulted in falling into empty arms.

# Speak What You Are Feeling

Speak what you are feeling! You matter, your words and feelings matter. Don't be afraid to speak your words. By being silent, those around you assume that you are excepting of how your days unfold. The quieter you are, the more you are allowing people to assume you are excepting the situation. Don't allow them to assume!

# We Know the Script by Heart

Beyond the lush, green alfalfa fields, to the mountain tops still in darkened shadows from the past night. We, the birds and I, could see a tiny twinkling of first light. We all were very anxious for our favorite star to appear. Then, as if a magic wand had been tapped onto the mountain tops, there she was! A performance that we, the birds and I, see every day. We know the script by heart, but we never get tired of seeing it and always look forward to tomorrow's show!

# Time

Time: there's never enough of it, and we always run out of it. It's time to go, time to get up, time to eat, sleep, work, time for school, and time to catch the bus, train, or plane. There's time to go home, make dinner, put kids to bed, put oneself to bed, and in no time, it's time to get up and do it all over again! We waste time, try to make time, and we have the time of our lives.

There's vacation time, sick time, downtime and our favorite time of the day, year or our life. There's no time like the present to take time to smell the roses, and we all know about the time that will heal all wounds. We live in a scheduled world; everything has its time!

Well, I think it's "time" to find some "time" away from a schedule and just "take our time!"

# Live

Don't get so caught up in making a living that you forget the "live" part!

# Use Your Mind

Make your decisions with more of a thinking mind and less with a grieving heart!

# My Truths

My truths are that I overreact to situations. I overthink just about everything, and as a mother, I overprotect or try to overprotect my grown children! When my kids were little, I always tried to give them a soft landing with whatever they were doing that may have been difficult or hurtful, and I was always there to kiss the bruises and rub the bumps. I think that the protection thing stays with you as a mother because even now that my kids are adults, I find myself still trying to protect and give them that soft landing in difficult situations, and it doesn't quite work the way it did when they were little. All of what I try to do still, as a parent, is always in love and concern, never to control or make anyone feel obligated to me in any way. So, I just want my adult children to know that I love them, and I support them in their choices. Also, I am here to help when they need me! That is all I can do!

# Just Do It!

My prescription for today and every day is:

Get Up
Get Dressed
Throw A Little Makeup On
Brush Your Hair (bedhead is not in style)
Brush Your Teeth
Stop Making Excuses
Live

# Past Nights Promise to Us All

The past nights promise to us all... first light!

# Let Your Heart Speak

Let your heart speak. Let your feelings be heard! Nothing was ever gained by being silent, except maybe smiles from your mother when you were quiet in church! There's no time to be quiet now. Let your heart tell it like it is! No holding back.

# Stillness

Stillness whispers the most beautiful song!

# Never Settle for What Is

If you know you always have options, your journey does not stop because life isn't as expected. You must never settle for what is; you must always push on to see what can be!

# Don't Erase Your Slate

I am changing the way I look at the continuation of years and my way of thinking when a "New Year" is presented to me! I have a hard time recognizing that the new year must come to me with a so-called clean slate. The thought that on January first, I must wipe my slate clean, leave the previous year behind me and start all over again pains me to my core. I've come up with a new way of identifying the new year, which is a new year, because my calendar tells me it is.

I would much rather think of the new year as a new life phase, a continuation of my journey, not an ending of my life as I have known it. I don't want to end my previous life phase by stripping myself of all that has transpired during that time and just forgetting it and moving on. I want to celebrate my accomplishments, learned lessons, and growth from my experiences from my past life phase. I want to add to my slate, not throw it away. So instead of looking at the new year as an end and then beginning all over again, I am embracing my new life phase as a continuation of my journey collecting more accomplishments, lessons and growth to add to my slate! Don't erase your slate!

# Sweet Perfect Harmony

The gentleness of the early morning is in sweet, perfect harmony with my soul!

# What A Beautiful Day

On my morning walk today, I was thinking about the wonderful morning walks I would take when I was living in the Florida Keys! Every morning, I passed by a little old man walking in the opposite direction from me. Like clockwork, every morning, he would smile at me, stretch his arms up towards the sky and say, "What a beautiful day." I would reply with a smile and say, "Yes, it is." On the return trip, we would pass by each other again, and as if he hadn't seen me before, he would smile at me, stretch his arms up towards the sky and say, "What a beautiful day." I would reply again with a smile, "Yes, it is." I don't know if he forgot that he had already seen me and said that, or if he just felt like saying it again, but he did this the same way every day. It was nice of him to share his happiness with me! What a difference it would make if people greeted everyone they encountered with that same joy! So, I say to you, "What a beautiful day!"

# Just Pray

When you are lost for words, don't know what to say, the simple answer is just to pray!

# Use Your Free Pass

The sunrise this morning was extraordinary. The star of the show was brilliant, and it looks like the show will be held over for a long time to come. The response from the theater patrons (the birds and I) has been outstanding. So, the show's producers, cast and crew have decided to extend this production for eternity! And, I might add, we've all been given free passes for every show! I hope you use your free pass!

# First Light Came Softly

The first light came softly, breaking into the darkness of the past night. Over the mountains and across the fields, shadows danced and disappeared into the light. Distant cooing from several mourning doves could be heard across the valley. In the stillness of these first moments of this brand new day, there was a feeling of new beginnings, new hope, and thankfulness for all my blessings.

# A Captured Fairy

On one of my early morning walks, I was trying to capture not only the beauty of the rising sun, but I was also trying to capture a little hummingbird that had landed on a branch in front of me. Upon looking at the picture when I returned home, it looked like I had also captured something else that I didn't see when I was taking the picture, and it looks like a little light with wings.

As I reviewed the picture a little more on the live setting on my phone, it showed that that light with wings had separate movement from everything else. As I reviewed the picture over and over again, I am convinced that I captured a picture of a fairy! I believe in fairies and angels and miracles and magic. I believe in God and love and Santa Claus. We should all believe in something and then watch the magic unfold!

# Shout To the Rooftops

Shout to the rooftops, sing to the sky, don't let anyone stop you, and I'll tell you why!

You are a beautiful woman (with a heart made of gold) that needs someone to love her, so I am told.

So, dance in the streets, and sing to the sky, don't let anyone stop you, and I'll tell you why!

Your happiness will shine through as you dance and sing, and others will see just what that will bring!

So, shout to the rooftops and sing to the sky, don't let anyone stop you, and I'll tell you why!

The fun and laughter that will soon appear will bring them all closer and bring them all near!

So, dance in the streets, and sing to the sky, don't let anyone stop you, and I'll tell you why!

Happiness will be yours from all that you do, a direct result of doing for you!

# Make It Happen

Whatever you are attempting to accomplish, don't stop until you make it happen! Good things come to those who work hard and don't give up.

# The Village by The Bay

I want to walk beside you along the shore of our favorite beach,
and climb the rocks of the jetty where the water cannot reach.
Let's find that woodland path again that we wandered down that day,
then take our chairs out to the dock and look out on the bay.
When morning comes, we'll head to town to our favorite coffee place,
white chocolate, raspberry scones for me, what a great taste!
What fun we'll have together in the village by the bay.
So glad we came to visit, so glad we came to stay!

# Trust

Nothing is holding you back.
Trust in the wind to carry you.
Trust in your wings to fly!

# One of the Chosen Ones

You were born to do great things, and those great things might not be what you think they are. The connection you have with God, the divine life force you feel surging through your veins, and the knowingness you have are all indicators of a higher purpose. Others see that life force within you, it is real, and it is a gift that was given to you to bring light, love, and healing to the world. So, you must continue to walk through the fires, brushing off the flames as you continue your journey to your purpose. You are one of the chosen ones; that is why so many roadblocks have appeared to you to help direct you away from what was not meant for you. And although there was much pain and sorrow, it wasn't to make you sad, but to make you strong, and it did. Go forward now, do your work, find your way, and present your gift to the world; they are all waiting!

# She Walks with Me

On my daily walks, I often think how wonderful it would be to have my mother walking beside me. Today, I realized that she is!

# She Never Felt Like She Belonged

She never quite felt like she belonged, no matter where her journeys took her. The only comfort that she could find was in his arms. Although his arms were not there for her all the time, and the love she felt for him was never returned to her, somehow, in those few and fleeting moments her heart beat next to his, and that was all that mattered.

# "I Promise I will Change"

People who say they will change refer to letting you know they will be more diligent in changing their underwear every day! Their attitude and personality are theirs for life; those things will never change. They are part of who they are and how they were raised. So, when someone says they will change, give a little thumbs-up, and then be on your way! They might be smelling better, but everything else will still stink!

# Peace And Harmony

Practice moments of peace! The dictionary describes peace as a state of quiet, freedom from disturbances, and being calm. The more you practice peace, the more your life will reflect calmness, and from calmness, harmony will be born. With the birth of harmony, you will then notice those little disturbances that previously bombarded your peace and took away your calmness no longer exist. Thus, you have now created peace and harmony!

# It's Okay If You're Not Feeling It!

You know it's okay if you're not feeling it! It's okay not to accept and fold into the flow if it isn't flowing for you! It's okay! It's no one else's concern but yours if it's not happening for you! You have no one else to answer to but yourself, and if you aren't happy, you need to fix that. No apologies, no explanations, no guilt. Make it right for you!

# Little Hands

The little hands that rearranged my Christmas Village have left to go back home. The giggles of joy and bright-eyed wonder have left me all alone. My house is back in order, and everything is in its place. All the remnants of their stay here are gone without a single trace.

# Do The Waves Still Crash Upon the Shore?

Do the waves still crash upon the shore when I'm not there to see? Are they lying in quiet stillness, just waiting there for me? Will the footprints that I left behind along that distant shore still be there when I return once more?

# Silently

Silently, the whispers of a distant wind call to me, beckoning me to come.

# Where I Am

Where I have been is where I had to be to get me to where I am!

# Songbird

You cannot stop a songbird from singing!

# No Directions

The negatives will never find their way into your life unless you give them the directions!

# What Will You Write?

The next page of your book of life has just arrived, what will you write?

# You Learn

You learn in having to…

# Don't Unpack Your Bags

Trying not to live in the past or at least reminisce all the time can be rather difficult for some people, as that is where their happiness was. Wanting to feel that happiness again, well, sometimes it's easier to look back, just don't unpack your bags!

# Why A Nest?

Why would I build a nest to keep all filled with twigs and trinkets when only I will see?

What calls to me to make a nest if only I am to be?

# My Beautiful Friend

This was my beautiful friend that flew in front of me and around me while I walked yesterday! He certainly wanted me to notice him, and I did! So thankful for simple pleasures that help keep you knowing that beauty and goodness are around if we just take the time to see and appreciate it.

# God's Way

There are disappointments in life; everyone has them! Disappointments are nothing more than God's way of directing you to something better! There is no roadmap to follow, but if you pay attention, you will find your way!

# Gypsy Blood

Yes, there is gypsy blood flowing through my veins, and that just means I enjoy adventure and freedom, and I welcome change! Every path that I have ever taken in this life's journey has always been taken with faith, hope, and excitement that that path was the right one. However, on very many occasions, it has not been the right path. And so, it seems that the one thing that I have discovered from taking the wrong path so many times, amazingly, is that I keep on trying again and again. So, although I have been at the depths of despair and seemingly not knowing what to do, I see another path, and I take it. Am I saying to myself after so much disappointment, "Why bother?" Yes, I am. In all honesty, yes, I am. But then comes that tapping on the shoulder, that curiosity, that glimmer of hope, that question, what if? What if this time, this path, this opportunity is the right one? So, like many times before, I grab my knapsack and keyboard and once again set out in search of the answer to "what if?"

# Written By a Great Master

The rhythm of the water harmonizing with the reflection of the sun is a composition written by a great master.

# The Passage of Time

Because of the passage of time, I am older now. Not a lot has changed except for a somewhat enhanced ability to really see things the way they truly are! I have always had a little edge on knowing, shall we say, some would call it intuition. However, I have not followed that knowing and have paid for it dearly in a couple of instances. I will not allow that to happen again. Some would say, I have learned my lesson! I would say "thank you" to my teachers.

# Write More Chapters

I see a lot of quotes that say let go of your past and I ask why? Your past was part of your journey, part of your life, part of you! So, maybe there were some things in your past that you wish you could forget, but you know what? You might be able to shut out those things, but they are still part of your journey. Part of what took place on your pathway that has gotten you here to this point of your life. So, I say, instead of letting go of your past, make peace with your past and embrace it as a necessary part of your story that helped you to write more chapters.

# Wonderful Aromas

There are wonderful aromas that fill my senses as I walk amongst the surrounding natural flora and fauna ever so abundant in early summer. The air is bursting with the sweet smell of cedar branches, honeysuckle, wild roses, and every now and then, the mossy smell of wet mulch and leaves that mix in the air with beach plum blossoms and salt air from the ocean! All are fond and memorable aromas that live on and become sweet nectar to my soul!

# Speak Softly

Speak softly to me in a loving way, for we may only have today!

# Music Is Everywhere

There is music in the air, in the raindrops, in the brook, in the ocean, in the leaves... listen!

# On The Other Side of That Door

There is life on the other side of that door; you can hear it taking place. The well-known sound of the garage door opening for the first to leave in the morning. Familiar, loving exchanges of morning words before they are off to start their day, one-by-one, off they go to work and school. And in great anticipation, I wait for nothing more than the time of day when I will hear the garage door opening again, this time, as one-by-one they return from their day in their life!

# Raise The Sails

The wind will blow anyway it wants to. It's up to you to raise the sails, catch the breeze, and enjoy the ride.

# The Magic of Love

The magic of love is love itself and the magical way it makes you feel! Thinking it will never end is not ignorant. Instead, it is the hope and faith you have in your heart and relationship that it will last forever. If love fails, then it just wasn't meant to be. The ignorance comes when we shut ourselves away behind walls after being hurt by love, not allowing ourselves to feel that magic again.

# Love Yourself

You already have it within you to be loving and caring. Stop giving it away to those who don't return it, and give some of it to yourself! Love yourself; it feels good!

# Change

C = Create

H = Happiness

A = And

N = New

G = Great

E = Enlightenment

# The Moments Before First Light

There is such peacefulness in the moments before the first light. The world is still and quiet; the air is crisp and fresh. The only sounds you hear are distant birds singing their happy songs and the whisper of a gentle breeze rustling through the trees.

The moments that you take to look up to the sky and marvel at the miracles around you are precious. I think if everyone took fifteen minutes out of their morning and just lost themselves in those moments before first light, the world would be a very different place.

# The Right Decision

You won't know if you've made the right decision until you make it. And whether wrong or right, if you don't take a chance, you will never know how it would have turned out!

# Other works by
# Deborah Thatcher Robbins

*Unspoken Words* A book of poems © 1996

*Journey Home, Silhouettes, Dancing with The Moon,* and *Visions of Nature* - CDs of Deborah's beautiful piano compositions.

Coming Soon, *A Mother's Thank You Notes to Her Children* ©

A beautiful book filled with sentiments of love from a mother's heart to her children. This book is sure to be a favorite of loving mothers everywhere!

*Note:*
Thank you for choosing me to be your mother! Thank you for being my little Angel!

*Note:*
Thank you for keeping me company during your journey to being born; I had a little companion for nine months, and I was never alone!

Coming Soon, *The Adventures of Becca and Nanas* ©

A children's series about a young child named Becca and the adventures she has with her Nanas, her grandmother. Together they have lots of fun and happy, memorable times!

Children ages 1-6 will enjoy reading these books or having them read to them, the pictures are fun and colorful, and the theme is always love and togetherness.